MEGA DINOSAURS

picthall and gunzi

an imprint of Award Publications Limited

ISBN 978-1-909763-33-3

First published 2019

Copyright © 2019 Picthall and Gunzi, an imprint of Award Publications Limited
The Old Riding School, Welbeck, Worksop, S80 3LR

All rights reserved. No part of this publication may be reproduced, stored in a retrieval system
or transmitted in any form or by any means, electronic, mechanical, photocopying, recording
or otherwise, without the prior written permission of the copyright owner.

Written and edited by: Nina Filipek
Designed by: Jeannette O'Toole

Images: (all Shutterstock unless noted) front cover: DM7, Photobank gallery; back cover: DM7, Jean-Michel Girard; p1: Leonello Calvetti; p3: Catmando, Twin Design, Michael Rosskothen, Elenarts, Vector Goddess, Elenarts, m.pilot, DM7, Leonello Calvetti, Valentyna Chukhlyebova, Michael Rosskothen, miha de; pp4–5: Michael Rosskothen, Linda Bucklin, Catmando, somyot pattana, Matt Antonino, Christian Delbert; pp6–7: Leonello Calvetti, Catmando, David Herraez Calzada, Twin Design, Marcio Jose Bastos Silva; pp8–9: Michael Rosskothen, Leonello Calvetti, dimair, Mikkel Bigandt; pp10–11: Elenarts, Linda Bucklin, Axente Vlad, Vector Goddess, Leonello Calvetti, m.pilot; pp12–13: Elena Schweitzer, DM7/Adobe Stock, Baciu; pp14–15: Michael Rosskothen, Linda Bucklin, Leonello Calvetti, Africa Studio, zcw, STILLFX; pp16–17: DM7, Michael Rosskothen, Leonello Calvetti; pp18–19: Michael Rosskothen, Leonello Calvetti, Catmando; pp20–21: Leonello Calvetti, Catmando, Michael Rosskothen; pp22–23: Jean-Michel Girard, Michael Rosskothen, Catmando; pp24–25: Elenarts, Michael Rosskothen, Leonello Calvetti; pp26–27: Lukasz Kurbiel, Valentyna Chukhlyebova, Michael Rosskothen, Leonello Calvetti; pp28–29: Michael Rosskothen, Catmando, Sombra; pp30–31: PandaWild, Elenarts, DM7, Catmando, miha de.

Please note that every effort has been made to check the accuracy of the information contained in this book, and to credit the copyright holders correctly. Picthall and Gunzi apologise for any unintentional errors or omissions and would be happy to include revisions to content and/or acknowledgements in subsequent editions of this book.

19 1

Printed in China

CONTENTS

Terrible Reptiles 4

Fossil Finds 6

First and Biggest 8

What We Know 10

Meat-eaters 12

Plant-eaters 14

Deadly Dinosaurs 16

Body Armour 18

Skulls and Spikes 20

Crests and Bills 22

Feathered Dinosaurs 24

Flying Reptiles 26

Sea Reptiles 28

Dinosaur Disaster! 30

Glossary 32

TERRIBLE REPTILES

Dinosaurs lived over 66 million years ago, at a time when the Earth was covered in forests, deserts and shallow seas. Some dinosaurs were much larger than animals that are alive today. For example, Diplodocus was almost as tall as two giraffes standing on top of each other!

Small head

Extremely long neck

Diplodocus
say it like this:
Dip-lo-doh-cus
or like this:
Dip-lod-er-cus

What does the word 'dinosaur' mean?

Can you point to?

an eye

a foot

a nostril

a tail

Giganotosaurus
Gi-gano-toe-saw-rus

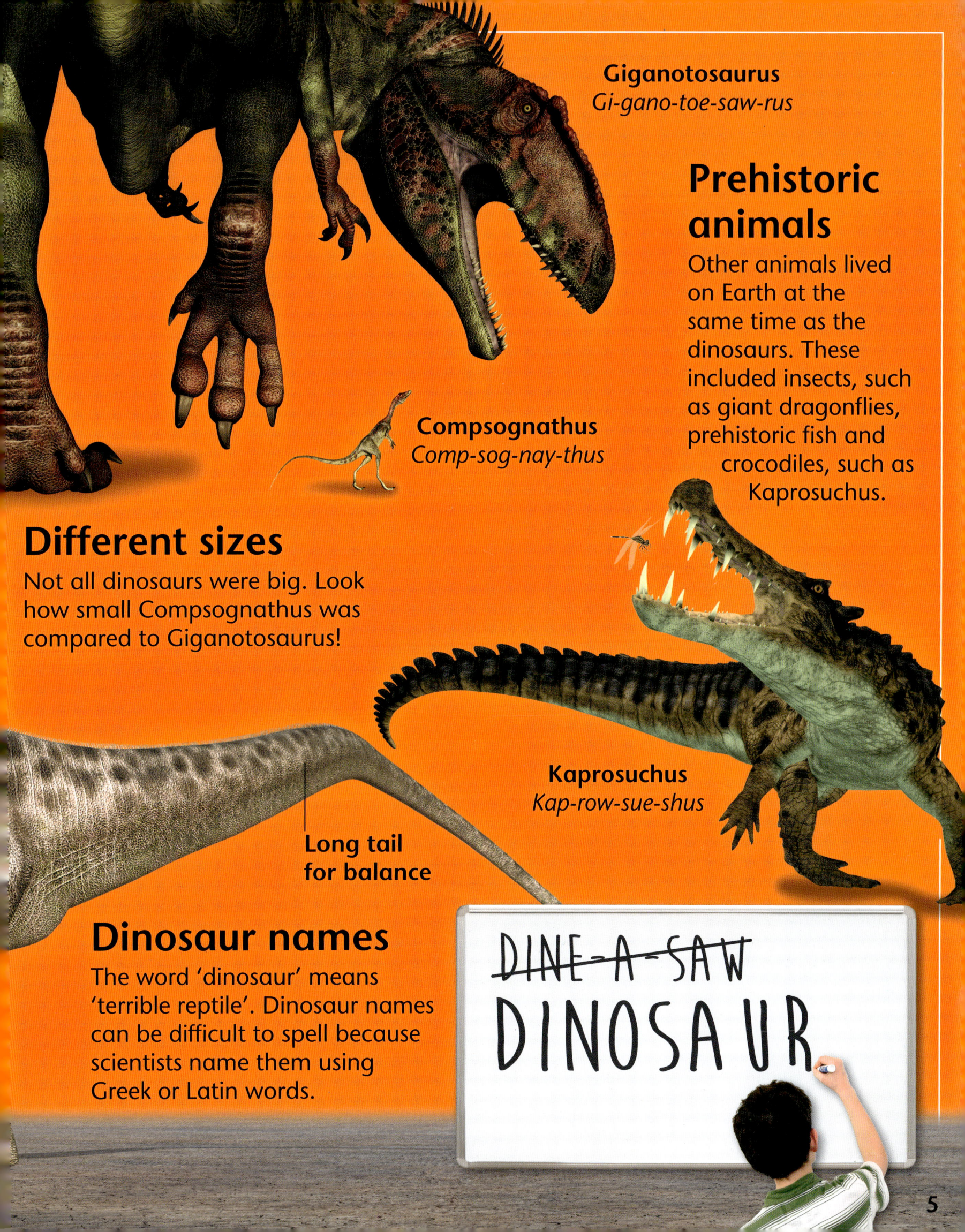

Prehistoric animals

Other animals lived on Earth at the same time as the dinosaurs. These included insects, such as giant dragonflies, prehistoric fish and crocodiles, such as Kaprosuchus.

Compsognathus
Comp-sog-nay-thus

Different sizes

Not all dinosaurs were big. Look how small Compsognathus was compared to Giganotosaurus!

Kaprosuchus
Kap-row-sue-shus

Long tail for balance

Dinosaur names

The word 'dinosaur' means 'terrible reptile'. Dinosaur names can be difficult to spell because scientists name them using Greek or Latin words.

FOSSIL FINDS

We know dinosaurs existed because their fossils have been found in many places around the world. A fossil is a bone, tooth or footprint that was buried in a layer of soft mud and, over millions of years, turned into stone.

Muscle modeling

When different bones from the same dinosaur are found, scientists can start to put them together to recreate its skeleton. Computer programs are used to add muscles and skin to the skeleton so we can see what the animal may have looked like.

Allosaurus
Al-o-saw-rus

This is what we think Allosaurus may have looked like, but we have no way of knowing what colour it really was!

Nostril

Tooth

Jaw

Nest egg

All dinosaurs started life in an egg. Fossil eggs have been found with baby dinosaurs inside them. Some dinosaurs laid as many as 20 eggs at a time.

Footprints

Sometimes we find dinosaur footprints. Millions of years ago, a dinosaur walked in some soft, sticky mud and left this footprint behind. We can see that it had three toes.

How are fossils made?

Eye socket

Skull

Tyrannosaurus rex
Tie-ran-o-saw-rus reks

Ribs

Leg

7

FIRST AND BIGGEST

The first dinosaur skeleton to be discovered and named was Megalosaurus, meaning 'great lizard'. Its bones were found in England in 1824. Since then, fossils from over 700 different kinds of dinosaurs have been found.

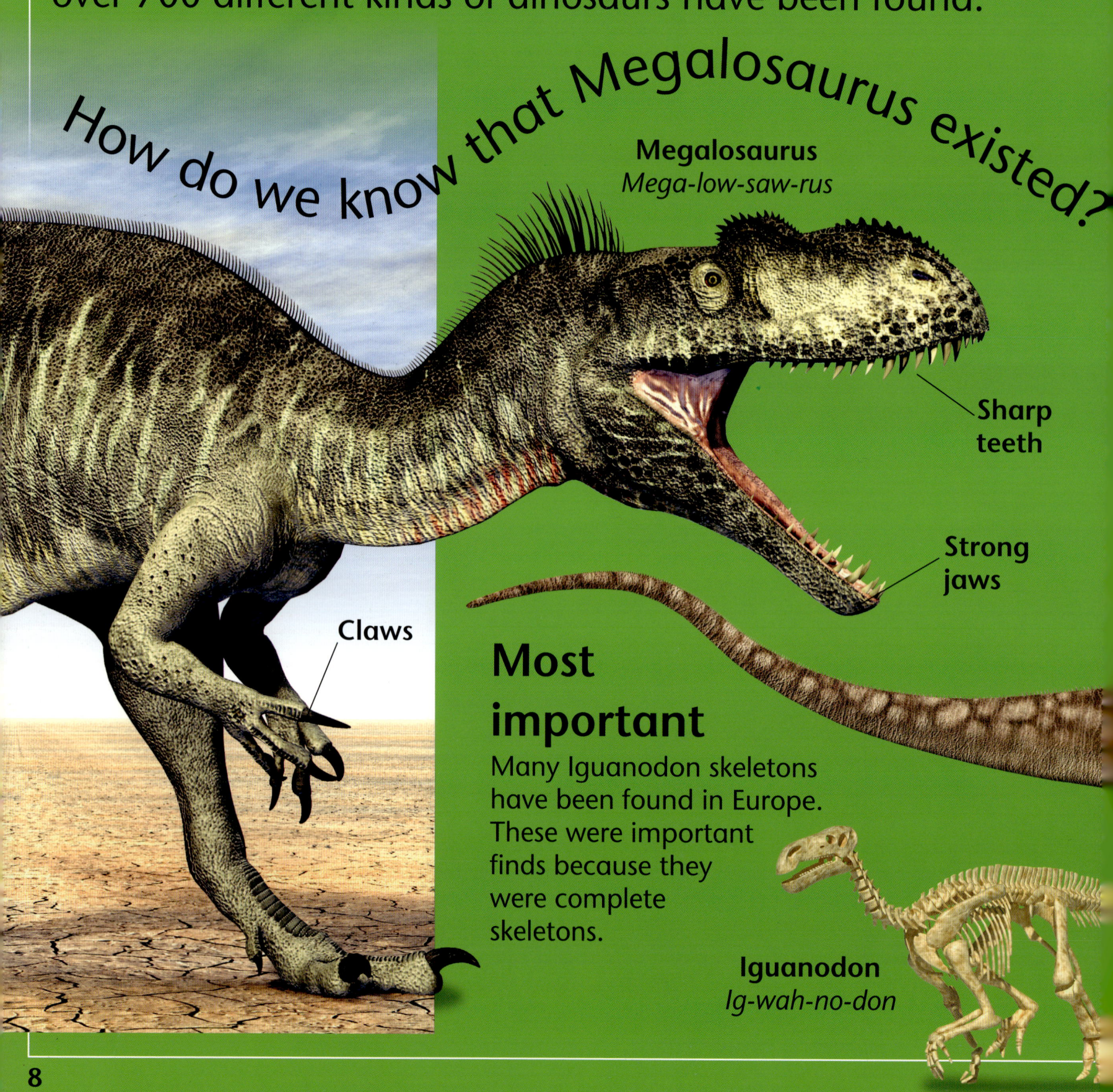

How do we know that Megalosaurus existed?

Megalosaurus
Mega-low-saw-rus

Sharp teeth

Strong jaws

Claws

Most important

Many Iguanodon skeletons have been found in Europe. These were important finds because they were complete skeletons.

Iguanodon
Ig-wah-no-don

Triceratops
Try-serra-tops

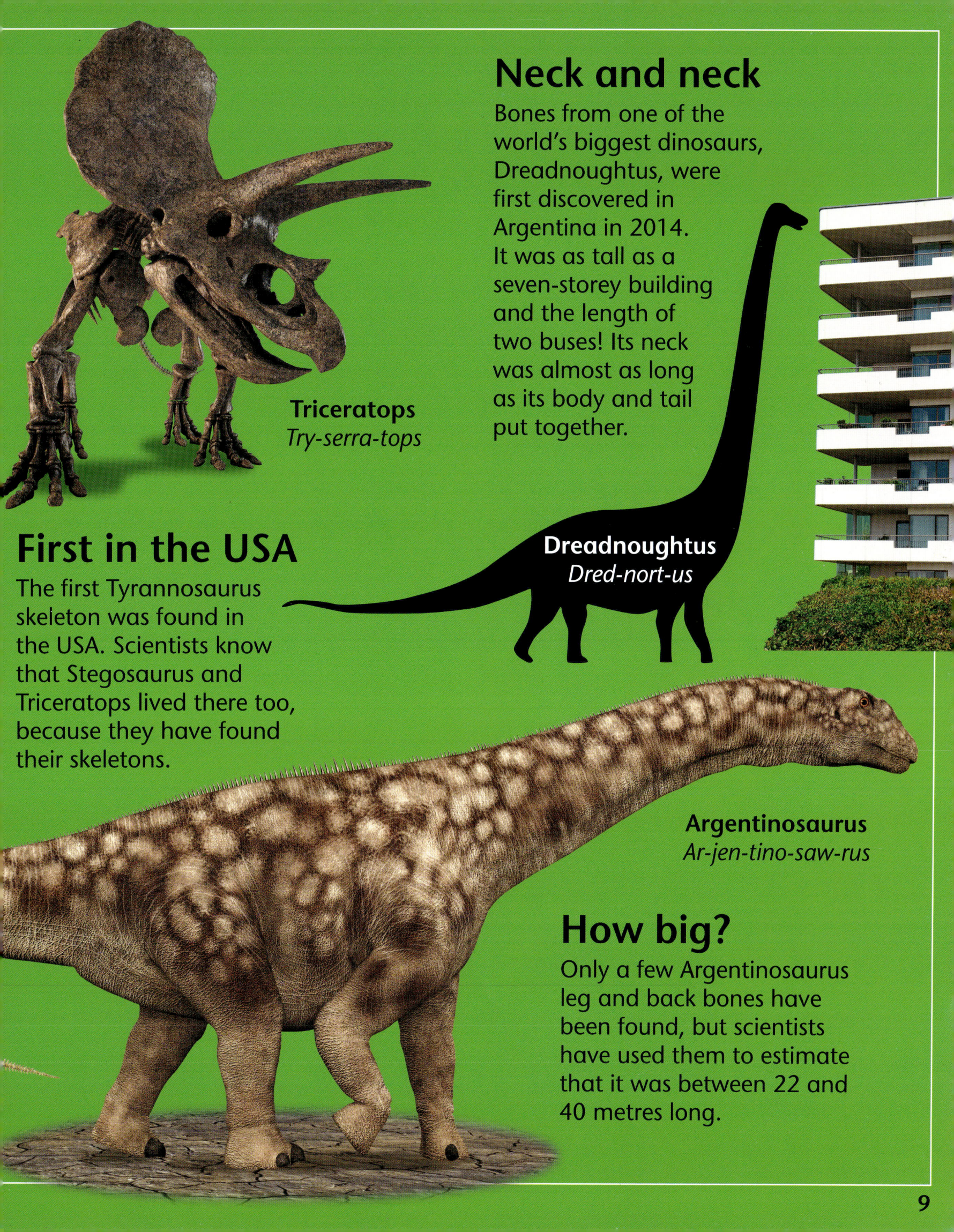

Neck and neck
Bones from one of the world's biggest dinosaurs, Dreadnoughtus, were first discovered in Argentina in 2014. It was as tall as a seven-storey building and the length of two buses! Its neck was almost as long as its body and tail put together.

Dreadnoughtus
Dred-nort-us

First in the USA
The first Tyrannosaurus skeleton was found in the USA. Scientists know that Stegosaurus and Triceratops lived there too, because they have found their skeletons.

Argentinosaurus
Ar-jen-tino-saw-rus

How big?
Only a few Argentinosaurus leg and back bones have been found, but scientists have used them to estimate that it was between 22 and 40 metres long.

WHAT WE KNOW

We know that some of the biggest dinosaurs had the smallest brains and were not very bright. Smaller dinosaurs, such as Compsognathus, had large brains for their size – they would have been clever and cunning.

Which dinosaur was clever?

Argentinosaurus
Ar-jen-tino-saw-rus

- Weighed as much as 12 adult African elephants!
- 22–40 metres long
- It had a small brain for a large dinosaur

Turkey

Compsognathus
Comp-sog-nay-thus

- Same size as a turkey
- 1 metre long
- It had a large brain for a small dinosaur

What colour were they?

Scientists don't know what colour many of the dinosaurs were, but some of them may have been brightly coloured to attract a mate, or the same colour as their surroundings to help them hide from other dinosaurs.

Stripes for camouflage

Maiasaura
Maya-saw-ra

What did dinosaurs eat?

The shape of a dinosaur's teeth can tell us what it was likely to eat. For example, some plant-eaters had flat teeth that were good for chewing, and meat-eaters had sharp teeth that were best for tearing flesh.

Meat-eaters had sharply pointed teeth

Spinosaurus
Spine-o-saw-rus

Dinosaur droppings!

Scientists can find out more about a dinosaur's diet by studying fossilised dinosaur poos, called 'coprolites'!

MEAT-EATERS

Meat-eating dinosaurs, or 'carnivores', had to be fast and fierce to catch a meal. They had powerful leg muscles for running, sharply-pointed teeth for biting and long claws for grabbing hold of prey.

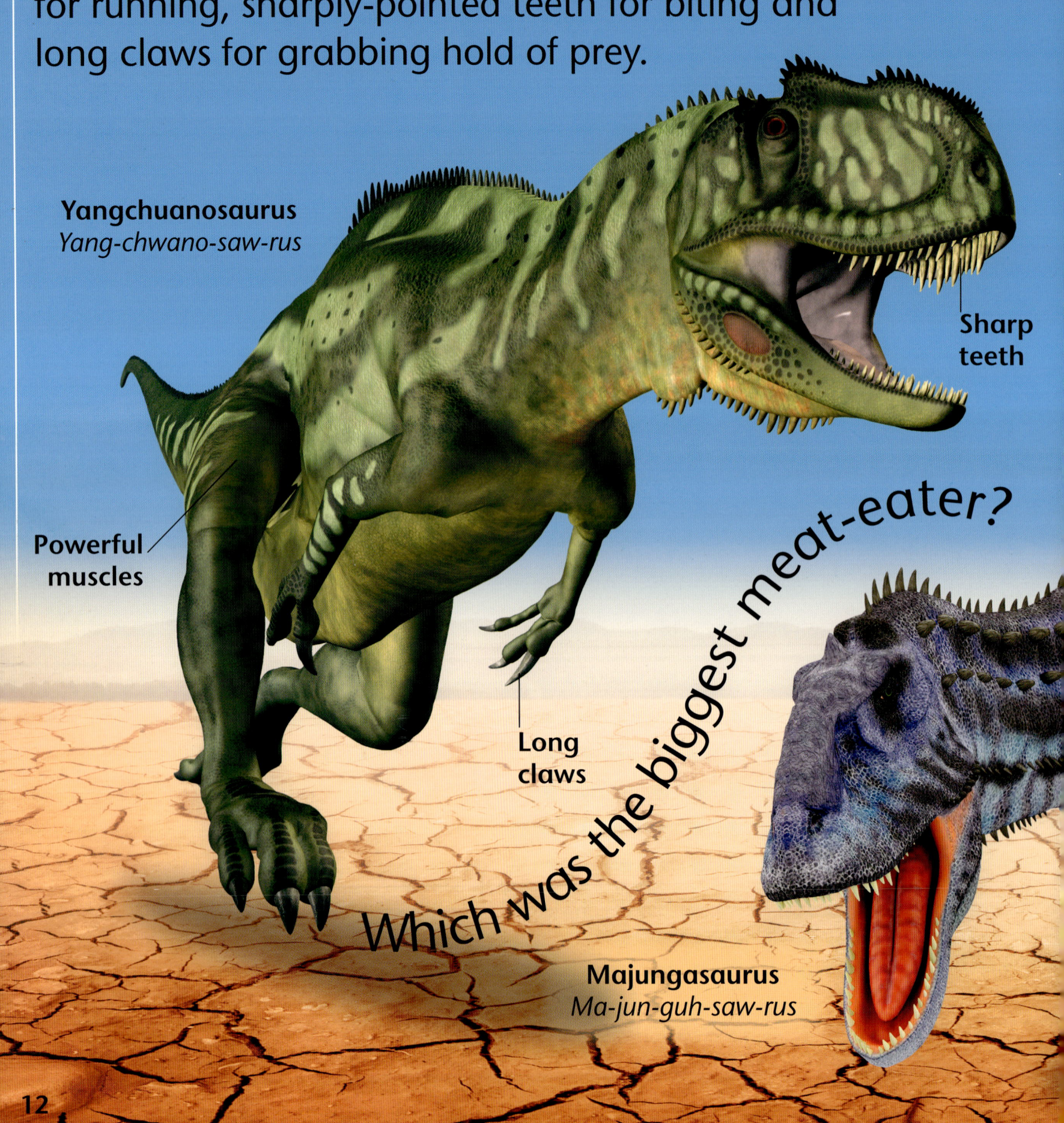

Yangchuanosaurus
Yang-chwano-saw-rus

Sharp teeth

Powerful muscles

Long claws

Which was the biggest meat-eater?

Majungasaurus
Ma-jun-guh-saw-rus

Insectivores

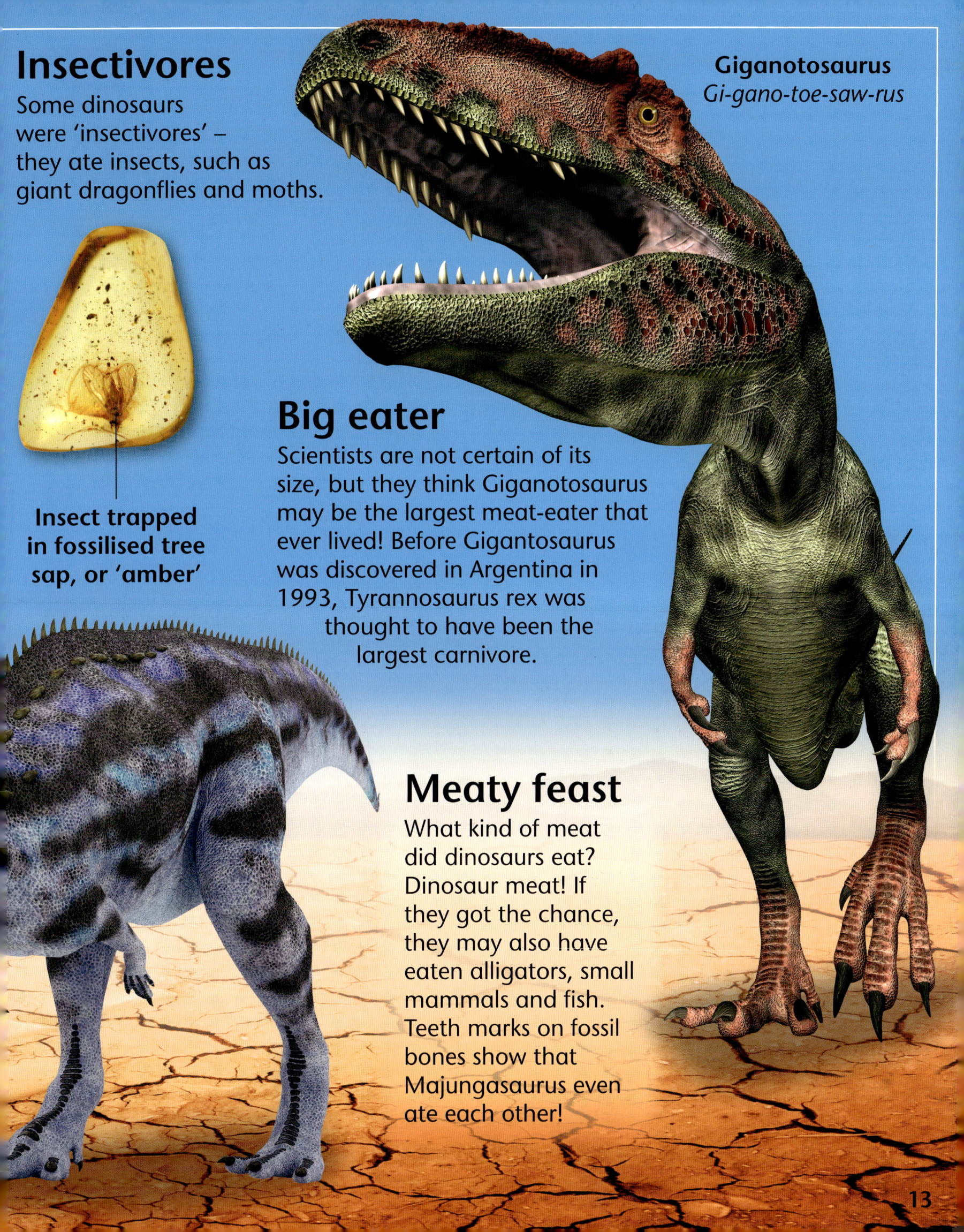

Some dinosaurs were 'insectivores' – they ate insects, such as giant dragonflies and moths.

Insect trapped in fossilised tree sap, or 'amber'

Giganotosaurus
Gi-gano-toe-saw-rus

Big eater

Scientists are not certain of its size, but they think Giganotosaurus may be the largest meat-eater that ever lived! Before Gigantosaurus was discovered in Argentina in 1993, Tyrannosaurus rex was thought to have been the largest carnivore.

Meaty feast

What kind of meat did dinosaurs eat? Dinosaur meat! If they got the chance, they may also have eaten alligators, small mammals and fish. Teeth marks on fossil bones show that Majungasaurus even ate each other!

PLANT-EATERS

Plant-eating dinosaurs, or 'herbivores', were often much bigger than meat-eaters. The biggest could not chew their food, so swallowed stones to grind it into smaller pieces to make it easier to digest. Their huge size made it harder for carnivores to attack them.

What did herbivores eat?

Europasaurus
Yoo-ro-pa-saw-rus

Can you point to?

an eye

a beak

bones

14

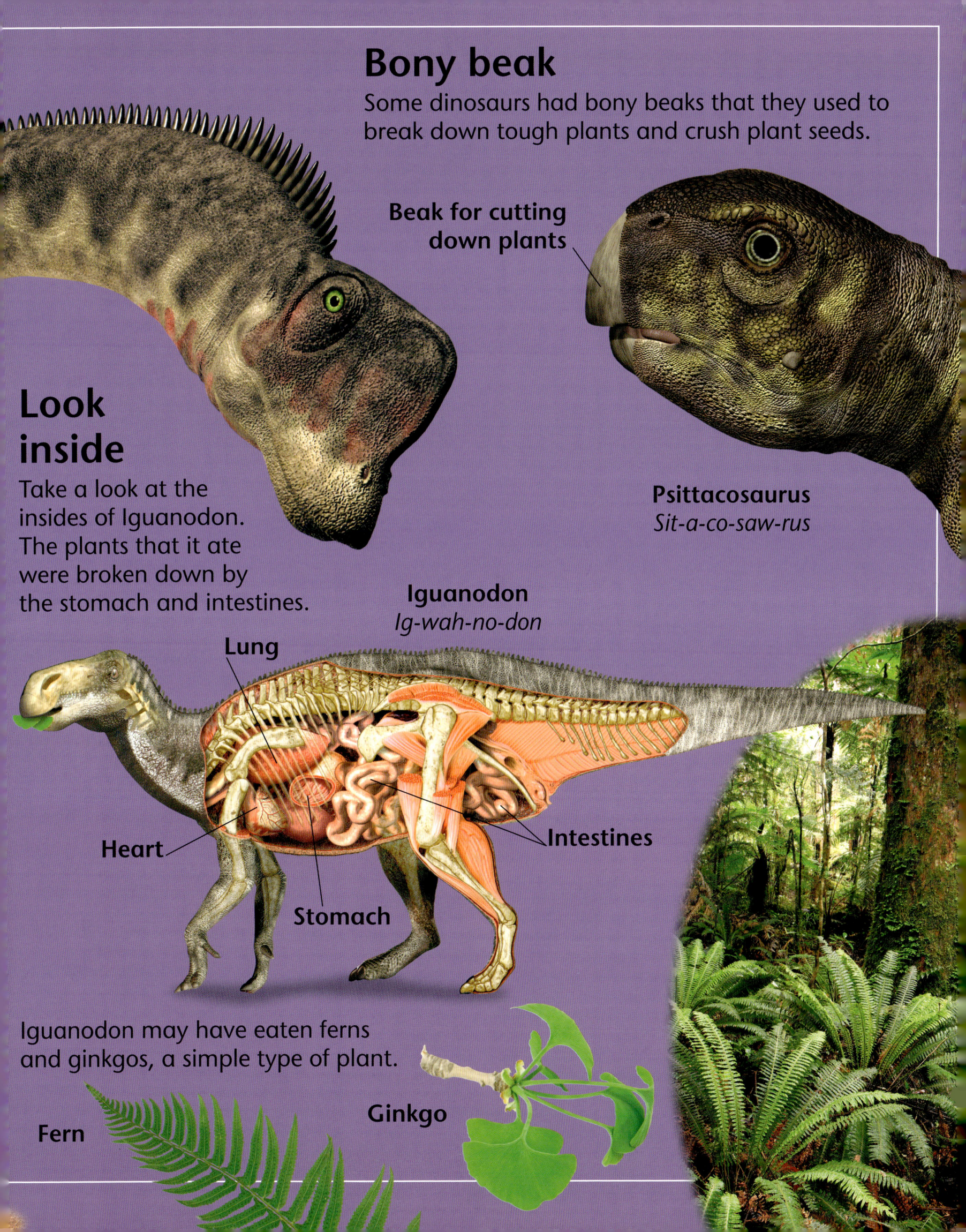

Bony beak
Some dinosaurs had bony beaks that they used to break down tough plants and crush plant seeds.

Beak for cutting down plants

Psittacosaurus
Sit-a-co-saw-rus

Look inside
Take a look at the insides of Iguanodon. The plants that it ate were broken down by the stomach and intestines.

Iguanodon
Ig-wah-no-don

Lung

Heart

Stomach

Intestines

Iguanodon may have eaten ferns and ginkgos, a simple type of plant.

Fern

Ginkgo

DEADLY DINOSAURS

Tyrannosaurus rex was a dinosaur with a massive bite! It had 60 sharp teeth set in its powerful jaws. It was longer than a big bus. With a good sense of smell, it could track down its prey from far away.

Tyrannosaurus rex
Tie-ran-o-saw-rus reks

Can you point to?

an eye

claws

teeth

Can you see its small arms?

Deinonychus
Die-noni-kus

No biting!
Triceratops used its sharp horns to fight with other triceratops and to defend itself from Tyrannosaurus. Its bony neck frill was used for protection. We know this because bite and horn marks have been found on its bones!

Claws and feathers
Scientists think Deinonychus had feathers, though it could not fly! Although its name means 'terrible claw', its fearsome-looking talons were better for climbing than attacking!

Triceratops
Try-serra-tops

Thorny lizard
Spinosaurus had a row of sharp spikes along its back for protection, and its 15–20 cm long curved claws were perfect for attack.

Spinosaurus
Spine-o-saw-rus

17

BODY ARMOUR

Plant-eating dinosaurs had to defend themselves from other dinosaurs who wanted to eat them. Some did this by using their body armour. Stegosaurus used the sharp spikes on its tail to fight off attackers.

Why did some dinosaurs have armour?

Small head

Stegosaurus
Steg-o-saw-rus

Walked on four legs

Can you point to?

a bony plate   a tail club   a horn

Tail club

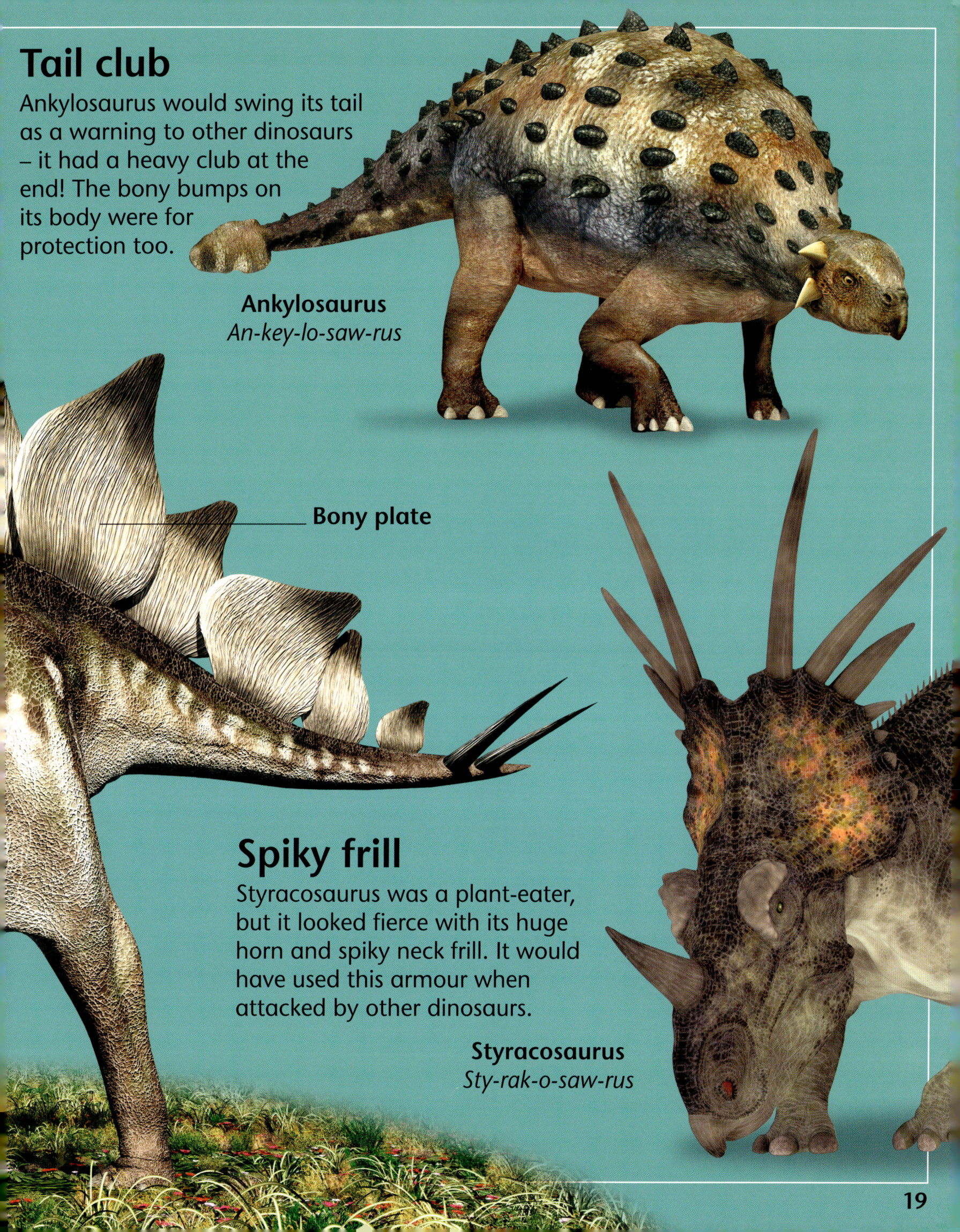

Ankylosaurus would swing its tail as a warning to other dinosaurs – it had a heavy club at the end! The bony bumps on its body were for protection too.

Ankylosaurus
An-key-lo-saw-rus

Bony plate

Spiky frill

Styracosaurus was a plant-eater, but it looked fierce with its huge horn and spiky neck frill. It would have used this armour when attacked by other dinosaurs.

Styracosaurus
Sty-rak-o-saw-rus

SKULLS AND SPIKES

Bone-headed dinosaurs lived in North America. They had big bony bumps on their heads that they used for ramming into the bodies of rival dinosaurs. Scientists don't think they clashed heads – that would have been far too painful!

Pachycephalosaurus
Pack-ee-seff-a-lo-saw-rus

Can you point to?

a mouth

a spike

an eye

Walked on two legs

20

How did this dinosaur use its head?

Skull dome
(up to 25 cm thick)

Blunt, bony spikes

Pointed beak

Spikey!

Kentrosaurus had two rows of plates and very long, sharp spikes along its back and down to its tail. The spikes made this small plant-eater look larger and more formidable.

Kentrosaurus
Kent-row-saw-rus

Gigantspinosaurus
Gi-gant-spine-o-saw-rus

Don't get too close!

Gigantspinosaurus had bony plates along the top of its body and one huge, curved spike on each shoulder. This warned other dinosaurs to stay away!

CRESTS AND BILLS

The long crest on the head of this duck-billed dinosaur had a hollow tube inside that was connected to its nose. By breathing air through the tube, this dinosaur could make a low sound to warn others of danger.

Parasaurolophus
Para-saw-rolo-fus

Do you think this dinosaur was fierce?

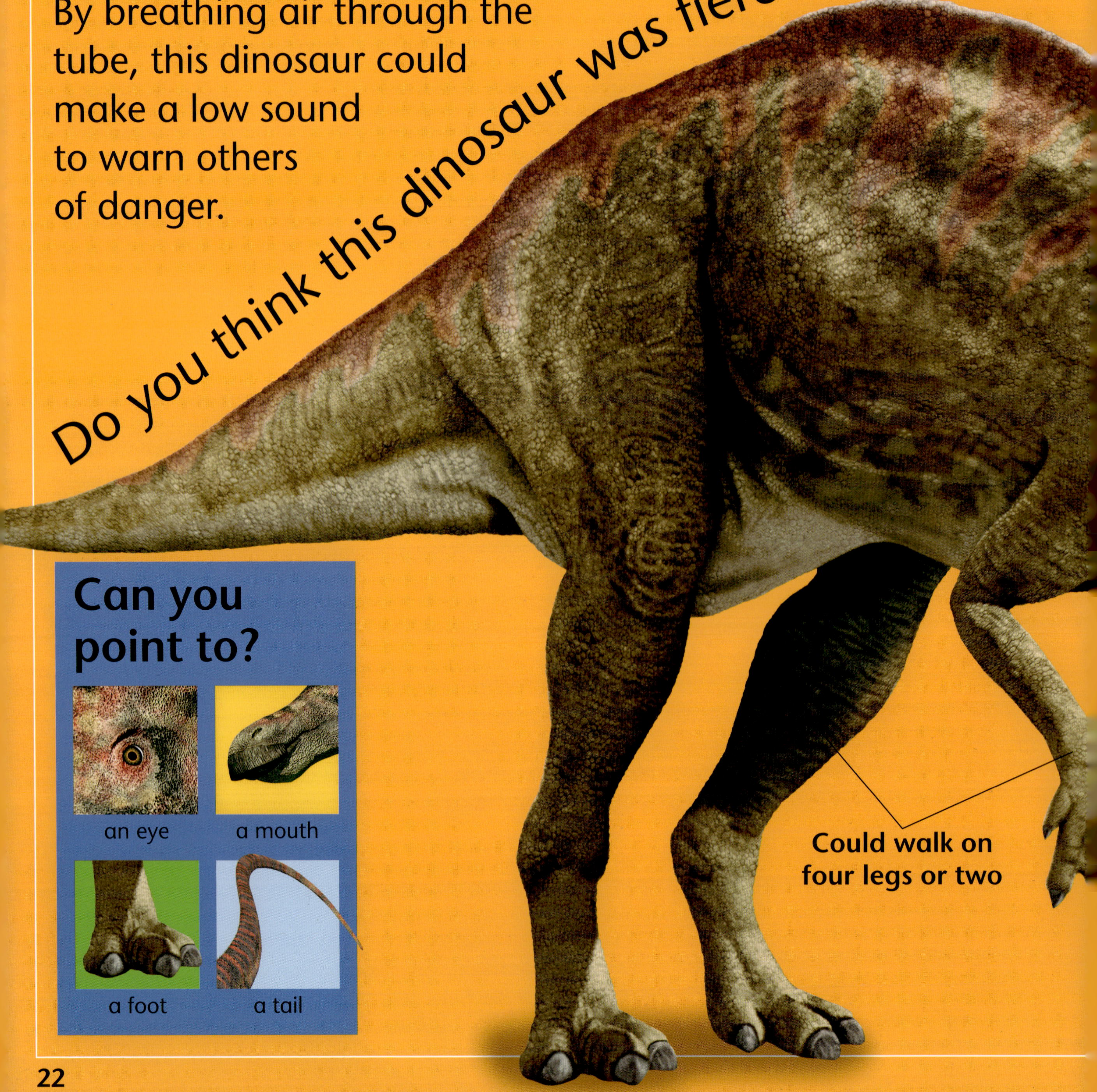

Could walk on four legs or two

Can you point to?

an eye

a mouth

a foot

a tail

22

Bony tube

Corythosaurus
Cori-tho-saw-rus

Mouth like a duck's bill

Dinner plates

Corythosaurus had a flat, round crest that looked like a dinner plate. This might have been used like an amplifier to make its call louder, or to help other dinosaurs recognise it.

Bony ridges

Dilophosaurus had two bony crests along the top of its head. These may have helped it to attract a mate.

Dilophosaurus
Di-low-fo-saw-rus

23

FEATHERED DINOSAURS

Some dinosaurs had feathers. This fast, feathered and toothless dinosaur was Gigantoraptor. Despite being almost the same height and weight as a giraffe, it could run quickly on its long legs, and its large claws made it a good hunter.

Do you think this dinosaur could fly?

Large eyes for good vision

Toothless beak

Gigantoraptor
Gi-gan-toe-rap-tor

Long, dagger-like claws

Long legs for running fast

Enormous eggs
Gigantoraptor stood 4 metres tall – and its eggs were giant too! At 45 cm long (about the same as one and half school rulers), they are among the largest dinosaur eggs ever discovered.

Feathery glider

This small reptile lived off the ground, in trees, for safety. With feathers on its arms and legs, it could glide from tree to tree.

Microraptor
My-crow-rap-tor

Velociraptor
Vel-o-soh-rap-tor

Speedy thief

Velociraptor's name means 'speedy thief'. Its feathers were probably used for courtship displays.

Early bird

Fossils of a small bird-like dinosaur called Archaeopteryx show bones, wings and feathers, though no one knows if they flapped their wings to fly or glided. Scientists think that some of the birds we see today could have evolved from Archaeopteryx.

Archaeopteryx
Ark-ee-op-ter-ix

25

FLYING REPTILES

While dinosaurs ruled the land, flying reptiles called 'pterosaurs' took to the skies. These reptiles were not dinosaurs, but they were close relations. They had long wings formed from skin and muscle stretched over thin finger bones.

Wings like a bat

Did this pterosaur have teeth?

Elongated 'finger' bone

'Fingers' on each wing

Rhamphorhynchus
Ram-for-in-kus

Wing finger

Like all pterosaurs, Rhamphorhynchus had large wings for soaring through the air. Can you spot its needle-like teeth and the diamond-shaped vane on its tail?

Head crest

Pteranodon
Ter-an-o-don

Toothless beak

Can you point to?

a foot

a wing tip

an eye

Fish-eater

Eudimorphodon's jaws were packed with 110 sharp teeth, including 6 sets of fangs. The shape of its teeth suggest that it would have eaten fish, which it would swoop down to snatch from near the surface of lakes and seas.

Eudimorphodon
Yoo-die-morf-o-don

SEA REPTILES

Scientists have found fossils of prehistoric sea creatures too. Some had long necks, and sharp teeth set in narrow, pointed jaws. These sea reptiles used their flippers like paddles to move quickly through the water.

Why did they have fins?

Long neck

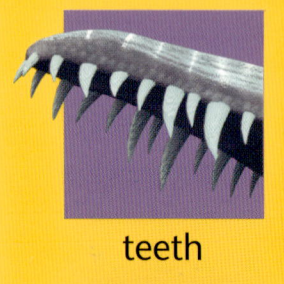

Thick body

Flipper

Tail

Can you point to?

teeth

an eye

a tail

Liopleurodon

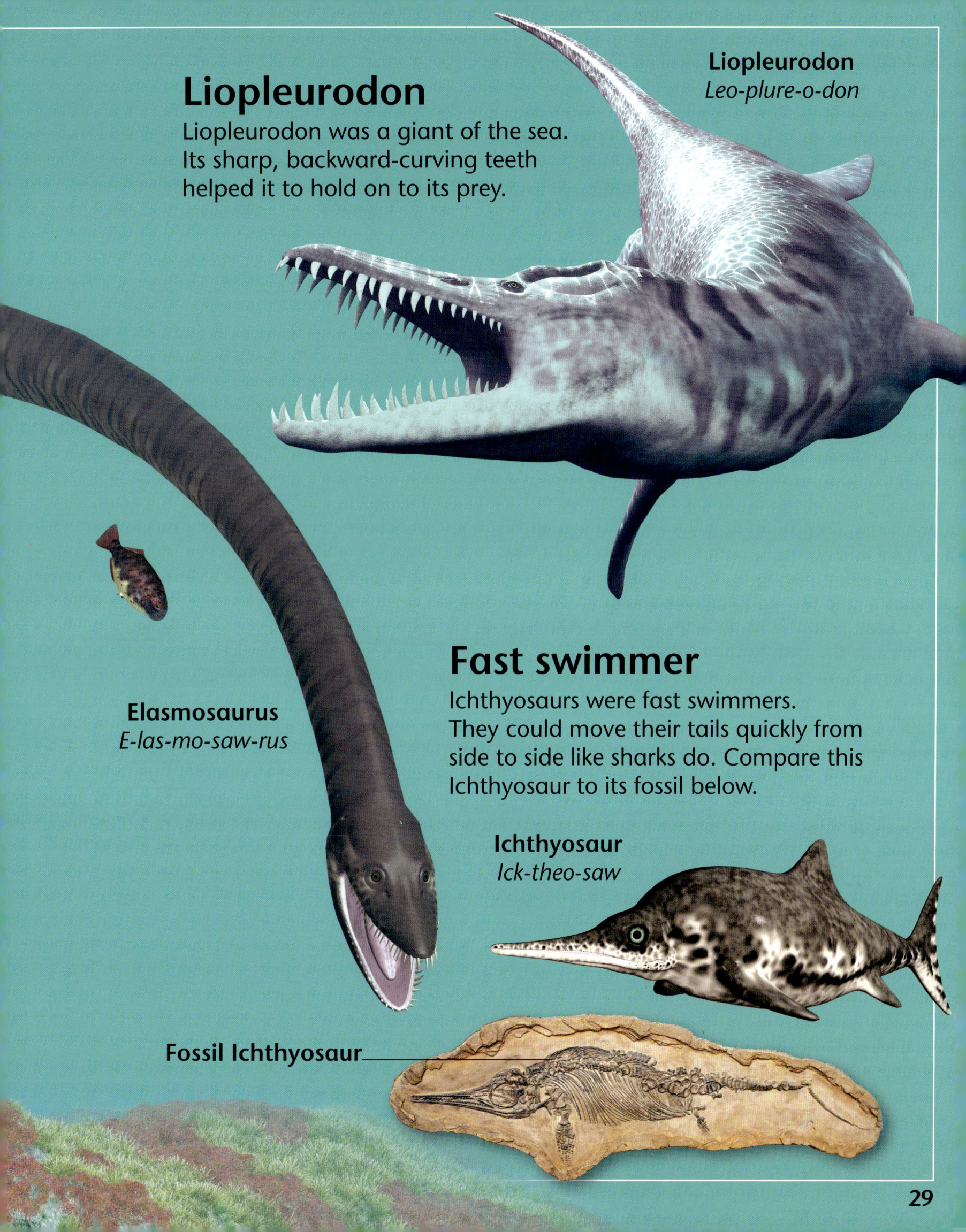

Liopleurodon was a giant of the sea. Its sharp, backward-curving teeth helped it to hold on to its prey.

Liopleurodon
Leo-plure-o-don

Elasmosaurus
E-las-mo-saw-rus

Fast swimmer

Ichthyosaurs were fast swimmers. They could move their tails quickly from side to side like sharks do. Compare this Ichthyosaur to its fossil below.

Ichthyosaur
Ick-theo-saw

Fossil Ichthyosaur

29

DINOSAUR DISASTER!

Dinosaurs, sea reptiles and pterosaurs were all wiped out by a huge disaster 66 million years ago. No one knows exactly what happened, but some scientists think that an enormous meteorite struck the Earth, which would have caused big changes to the atmosphere, killing many animals and plants – and making the dinosaurs become extinct.

Can you name this dinosaur?

Violent volcanoes

Other scientists say that huge volcanic eruptions threw millions of tonnes of rocks, hot lava and poisonous ash clouds into the air, killing the dinosaurs.

Climate change

Some scientists believe that the Earth became much colder and this killed the plants, along with the plant-eating dinosaurs. Eventually, the meat-eaters died too, when their source of food ran out.

Meteorite (a rock falling from space)

Poisonous gas clouds

Lava (molten rock)

Survivors!

Even though the dinosaurs died out, we know that many smaller animals survived, including birds, insects, crocodiles, lizards, snakes, and mammals – such as the insect-eating Morganucodon, which was the size of a mouse. Many of these survivors have developed and evolved into the animals found on Earth today.

Fur

Long whiskers

Claws for digging and burrowing

Morganucodon
Mor-gan-u-co-don

31

GLOSSARY

Camouflage – a pattern on an animal's skin that helps it to blend in with its surroundings.

Carnivore – a creature that only eats other animals, usually herbivores.

Courtship – what an animal does to attract a mate, so that they can make babies together.

Digest – to break down food in your tummy (particularly the stomach and small intestine), so that vitamins and nutrients can be used by your body.

Extinct – an animal or plant becomes extinct when all of its kind have died. Once that happens, the species is lost for ever and cannot be brought back to life.

Fossil – the impression or remains of a prehistoric plant or animal that have been preserved in rock.

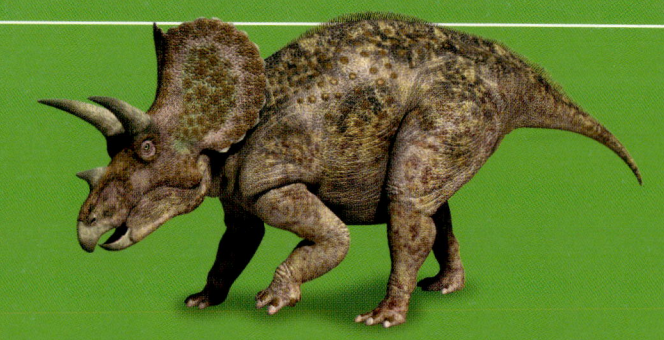

Herbivore – a creature that only eats plants.

Mammal – a warm-blooded animal that gives birth to live young instead of eggs. Humans are mammals.

Predator – an animal that hunts other animals.

Prehistoric – from a long, long time ago, before anything was written down.

Prey – an animal that is hunted by another animal.

Reptile – a cold-blooded creature that lays eggs and has dry, scaly skin.

Rival – a competitor for the same thing. Your friend could be your rival in a running race.

FIND THE PAIRS

Can you find all the matching pairs?

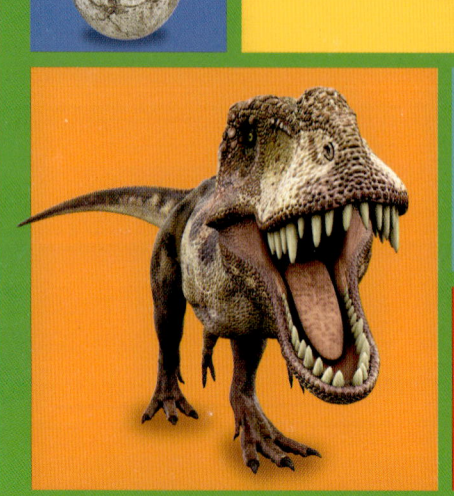